Robert Munsch

My Favorite Writer

Heather Kissock

Flint River Regional Library

WEIGL PUBLISHERS INC.

Published by Weigl Publishers Inc.
350 5th Avenue, Suite 3304, PMB 6G
New York, NY 10118-0069

Website: www.weigl.com

Library of Congress Cataloging-in-Publication Data

Kissock, Heather.
 Robert Munsch : my favorite writer / Heather Kissock.
    p. cm.
  Includes index.
  ISBN 978-1-59036-924-1 (hard cover : alk. paper) -- ISBN 978-1-
59036-925-8 (soft cover : alk. paper)
  1. Munsch, Robert N., 1945---Juvenile literature. 2. Authors, Canadian--
20th century--Biography--Juvenile literature. I. Title.
  PR9199.3.M818Z75 2008
  813'.54
  [B 22]

                                                          2008003969

Printed in the United States of America
1 2 3 4 5 6 7 8 9 0 12 11 10 09 08

Project Coordinator
Heather C. Hudak

Design
Terry Paulhus

All of the Internet URLs given in the book were valid at the time of
publication. However, due to the dynamic nature of the Internet, some
addresses may have changed, or sites may have ceased to exist since
publication. While the author and publisher regret any inconvenience this
may cause readers, no responsibility for any such changes can be accepted
by either the author or the publisher.

Contents

Robert Munsch

MILESTONES

1945 Born on June 11 in Pittsburgh, Pennsylvania

1960s Studies to become a **Jesuit** priest

1969 Graduates from Fordham University with a Bachelor of Arts in history

1971 Receives his **master's degree** in **anthropology** from Boston University

1973 Earns his master's degree in child studies from Tufts University and gets married

1975 Moves to Canada and teaches at the University of Guelph

1979 His first book, *Mud Puddle,* is published

1986 *Love You Forever* is published

1994 The New York Times lists *Love You Forever* as the best-selling children's book of all time

To write children's books well, it is good to be a big kid yourself. Robert Munsch proves this every time he writes a book. This author is a kid at heart. As a result, he is one of the world's most successful children's authors.

Robert brings enthusiasm to everything he writes. His stories put children in weird and wacky situations. Angela flies an airplane in *Angela's Airplane*. Megan lets the pigs out of their pen in *Pigs*. Life is an adventure for the characters in his books and the people who read them.

Robert Munsch connects with children's hopes and fears in a way few people can. His characters are smart, brave, and independent thinkers. Robert's love for children and for storytelling are always present in his books, which have been **translated** into many languages and have sold more than 30 million copies worldwide.

Early Childhood

Robert Munsch was born on June 11, 1945, in Pittsburgh, Pennsylvania. His father was a lawyer, and the family lived in a large farmhouse just outside the city. The Munsch family was large. Robert was the fourth of nine children. He had five brothers and three sisters. Growing up in a large family provided Robert with the ability to understand different types of people. This would help him later in his writing career, as he created unique characters.

Robert found school difficult. He was well-behaved in class, but he daydreamed often. He has said that the only reason he passed each grade was because no one wanted him to be in the same grade as his younger brother.

■ More than 316,000 people live in Pittsburgh.

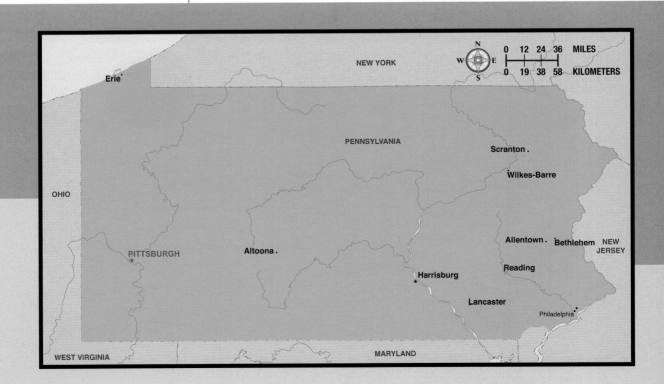

Throughout his elementary school years, Robert wrote poems, which often were funny. No one, including Robert, paid much attention to the poems at the time. However, one person at school took special notice of Robert's interest in reading and writing. The school librarian, Sister Emma Jean, encouraged Robert to read books and even had him help her in the library. They worked together to **catalog** library books. Robert visited Sister Emma Jean often. Having Sister Emma Jean believe in him helped him feel good about himself.

Like Robert, many students find the school library a good place to study and research projects.

Growing Up

"After all, while I made the best stories in the daycare centre, most of the other teachers made better playdoh."
Robert Munsch

In high school, Robert continued to find it difficult to learn. His teachers believed he was an intelligent boy, but they were unable to help him improve his mathematics and writing skills. At the same time, Robert's moods often shifted from happy to sad. He found comfort in reading. Books became his friends.

Jesuit priests belong to the Roman Catholic faith. They teach others the word of God.

When Robert finished high school, he became a Jesuit priest. While Robert was training to be a priest, he went to university. He graduated with a degree in history and then went on to earn a master's degree in anthropology.

The Jesuits are active in the communities they serve, and Robert looked for ways to help others. Even though he was busy studying, Robert found time to work at a local **orphanage**. There, he discovered that he liked being around children and that they liked being around him.

Robert trained to be a priest for seven years. However, when he was 25, Robert was attacked by a mugger and left with serious injuries. He decided to leave the Jesuits for a year.

Robert's work at the orphanage led him to take a job in a daycare center. It was here that he met his future wife, Ann. Ann was working at the daycare while studying for a degree in child studies. They met while changing a young girl's dirty diaper. Ann was touched by the way Robert handled children, and the two began dating.

Inspired to Write

Robert often develops stories about the children he meets. He asks them if they want to volunteer to have a story made up about them. Once he gets a name, he starts creating a story right on the spot. Sometimes, these stories become books.

More than 30 percent of children under age five whose mothers work, attend daycare, preschool, or nursery school.

Robert enjoyed working with young children and went back to university to learn more about them. During his studies, Robert became aware of his storytelling abilities. One day, while teaching at a preschool, he made up a story to tell the children. They loved it. This story later became one of his best-known books, *Mortimer*.

Robert received his master's degree in child studies in 1973. He and Ann married that same year. They spent the early years of their marriage working in daycare centers in different parts of the United States. All the while, Robert practiced his storytelling skills with audiences of eager children. In 1975, he and Ann moved to the province of Ontario in Canada, so that Robert could take a job at a university. He taught students about caring for young children. He also ran a preschool. It was an ideal environment for Robert, and he added more stories to his ever-growing collection.

Robert practices telling his stories many times. When he feels they are very good, he writes them down. He says this process takes about five years.

Robert's life was on a steady course. He had a happy marriage and a fulfilling job. However, his moods continued to swing. Ann suggested that Robert go to a doctor. The doctor found that Robert had **bipolar disorder**. The condition is treatable, and Robert's moods were brought under control with medication.

Robert was now ready to reach his full **potential**. Both adults and children enjoyed his storytelling. Many people urged Robert to write his stories down and try to get them published. At first, Robert ignored their comments. However, over time, he decided to give writing a try.

Guelph is home to one of only two covered bridges in Ontario. The lattice-covered bridge over Speed River was built in 1992.

Favorite Books

As a child, Robert often struggled with his feelings. There were times he was extremely happy and times when he was very **depressed**. He escaped from the bad times by reading all kinds of books. Robert was a big fan of books by Dr. Seuss, which are based on rhymes. The stories are often silly and have strange characters. Some of his better-known books are *The Cat in the Hat*, *Green Eggs and Ham*, and *The Grinch Who Stole Christmas*. Robert's favorite Dr. Seuss book was *The 500 Hats of Bartholomew Cubbins*.

Learning the Craft

Most authors start their writing careers by writing. They jot down their ideas and keep working on them until the words say exactly what the author means. Only when the author feels the story is at its best does it get made available to read.

Robert's writing career came only after he had been telling stories to children for more than 10 years. In a way, all of this storytelling was practice for Robert. He was learning how to write stories by telling them to the children who would be reading them in books. For this reason, he says, "I got it backwards!"

At first, Robert just wanted to entertain the children who were in his care. He did this through storytelling. Years of storytelling provided Robert with the opportunity to find out what children liked and did not like in a story.

> "Literacy is so important and it should be a family affair."
>
> **Robert Munsch**

Robert was 35 years old when he wrote his first book.

By watching the reactions of his audience, Robert was able to refine his stories after each telling. He would see what parts bored the children and what parts really interested them. He would then think of other ways to tell the story—what to take out, what to keep in, and what to change. Each time he told the story, it would change slightly. Robert would see how the children reacted to the revised story. If there were parts that still did not interest the children, he would make more changes and try telling it again. Sometimes, it was years before Robert was happy with the way children reacted to a story.

Inspired to Write

Robert believes that learning to write is similar to learning how to swim. People do not learn how to swim by reading about it. Likewise, a person will not learn how to write by reading a book that tells them how to write. In both cases, it is best to learn by doing it. "Practice makes perfect," and Robert believes that if people want to be writers, they should write as often as possible. Their writing skills will improve the more they practice.

Robert enjoys visiting schools and talking to children whenever possible.

Getting Published

Robert's storytelling abilities became known throughout the university where he taught. One day, the wife of Robert's boss visited the daycare where Robert worked. She was a children's librarian, so she was very interested in learning more about Robert. She listened while he told the children some of his stories. Afterwards, she told Robert that he should write his stories down and try to get them published.

Soon after her visit, Robert's boss began talking to Robert about getting his stories published. He gave Robert two months off from work to write. Robert waited until the end of the two months to begin writing. He quickly jotted down 10 of his stories and sent them to several publishing companies. He did not expect to receive any replies. One publisher responded favorably, and Robert's first book, *Mud Puddle*, was printed.

The Publishing Process

Publishing companies receive hundreds of **manuscripts** from authors each year. Only a few manuscripts become books. Publishers must be sure that a manuscript will sell many copies. As a result, publishers reject most of the manuscripts they receive.

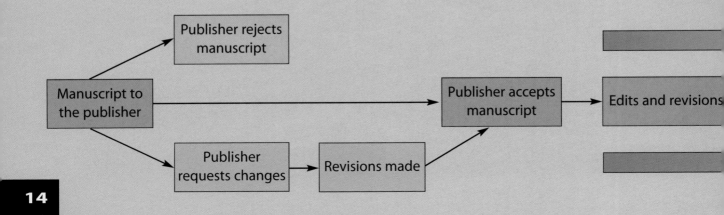

14

Mud Puddle was about a puddle that jumped on a boy. The book sold 3,000 copies in its first year. The publisher was happy with the sales and started publishing more of Robert's books. Over time, Robert's **reputation** as a talented writer grew, and his books became popular with children all over North America. Robert left his position at the university to write full time.

Inspired to Write

Ann has helped Robert develop his stories. One of the stories Robert told children was a fairy tale about a princess who was rescued by a prince. When Ann heard the story, she told Robert that women today do not need men to rescue them. Robert changed the story so that the princess rescued the prince. This story later became a book called *The Paper Bag Princess*.

Once a manuscript has been accepted, it goes through many stages before it is published. Often, authors change their work to follow an editor's suggestions. Once the book is published, some authors receive royalties. This is money based on book sales.

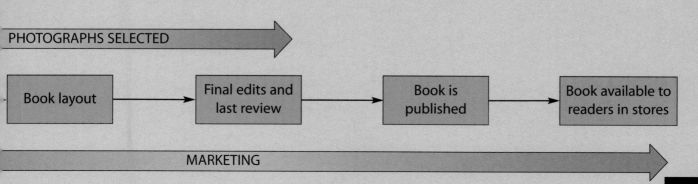

PHOTOGRAPHS SELECTED →

Book layout → Final edits and last review → Book is published → Book available to readers in stores

MARKETING →

Writer Today

Many of the children in Robert's books are based on real people. However, all of his stories are fictional, or make believe.

Robert and Ann Munsch continue to live in Ontario, Canada. They **adopted** three children—two girls and a boy—in the early years of their marriage. Robert's children, Julie, Andrew, and Tyya, are now adults. Robert continues to write books and has more than 40 titles in print. He tries to write two books each year.

Storytelling still plays a key role in Robert's life. He loves to hop in his car and travel to schools, daycares, and libraries to tell stories to children. Robert often arrives without notice and surprises everyone. He makes more than 200 appearances each year, including speeches to adult audiences.

Robert and his books have been recognized in a variety of ways. An audiotape reading of *Murmel, Murmel, Murmel* won a **Juno Award** in 1985. A year later, *Thomas' Snowsuit* was awarded the Canadian Booksellers Association's Ruth Schwartz Award for best children's book. The Canadian Author's Association awarded Robert the Vicki Metcalf Award for Children's Literature in 1987. In 1992, the Canadian Booksellers Association named Robert the "Author of the Year." The year 1999 was a very special year for Robert. He was awarded the Order of Canada. The Canadian government gives this honor to people who have had outstanding achievements in their field of work.

Robert has many more stories to tell. He has at least 200 stories in development.

Robert enjoys entertaining people.

Popular Books

All of Robert Munsch's books are popular. Children and parents seem to love everything he publishes. While most of Robert's stories sparkle with humor and spunky characters, they also show sensitivity to people's feelings and experiences.

AWARDS
Murmel, Murmel, Murmel

Juno Award 1985

Love You Forever
Before Robert and Ann adopted their three children, they had two babies that died. Robert wrote *Love You Forever* as a tribute to his children and the love that parents and children have for each other. The story follows the relationship of a mother and son. The relationship has happy and sad times as the boy grows up, but the mother's love remains constant. The son returns this love and passes it on to his own child later in life.

Murmel, Murmel, Murmel
One day, Robin is playing in her backyard when she hears a funny sound coming from a hole in the ground. When she investigates, she finds a baby in the hole. Robin knows that she is too young to take care of a baby, so she tries to find someone who will. The story follows Robin as she meets potential parents.

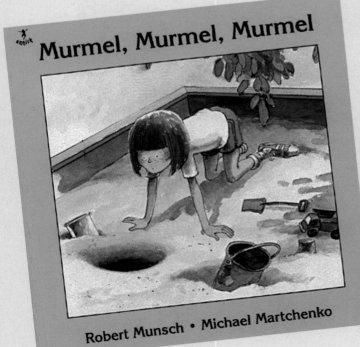

Murmel, Murmel, Murmel

Robert Munsch • Michael Martchenko

Thomas' Snowsuit

Thomas' mother buys him a new snowsuit for winter. Thomas thinks the snowsuit is UGLY, and he will not wear it. He refuses to wear it for his mother. He refuses to wear it for his teacher. He even refuses to wear it for the school principal. What makes him finally put it on?

Mortimer

It is time for bed, but Mortimer does not want to sleep. He wants to sing! However, no one wants to hear him sing. They want him to go to sleep. Their attempts to get Mortimer to go to sleep lead to even more noise. Does Mortimer ever fall asleep?

AWARDS
Thomas' Snowsuit

Ruth Schwartz Award 1986
Book Award Winner

David's Father

In this story, Julie makes friends with a boy named David. David seems like a nice boy, but Julie notices very strange things about the place where he lives. One day, David invites Julie into his house. Once inside, she learns that David's family is very different from her own. Julie discovers ways to embrace these differences.

Makeup Mess

Julie has saved up her money to buy makeup so that she can be pretty. She brings home the makeup and puts it on, but no one likes the way she looks. She decides to try again, but it does not look any better. People seem to think she looks better without the makeup, so Julie decides to stop wearing it. The problem is…she still has the makeup, and she spent her savings on it. Julie needs to get back her money, so she comes up with a plan.

Andrew's Loose Tooth

Andrew has a loose tooth that is not quite ready to come out of his mouth. It creates problems for Andrew whenever he wants to eat, and he wants it out of his mouth. His mom tries to get it out for him, but it will not come free. His dad tries to help, too, but with no luck. Other people try as well, but the tooth stays put. What can be done to help poor Andrew?

Something Good

When Tyya goes shopping with her Dad, she decides to show him how to shop for "good" food and loads up the cart with cookies, sodas, chocolate bars, and ice cream. Tyya's Dad gets mad at her, plants her in place, and tells her not to move. Unfortunately, a store clerk thinks she is a doll and tries to sell her. Tyya gets the last laugh, however, when her father tries to take her home.

Creative Writing Tips

R obert Munsch approaches the process of writing from an **oral perspective**. He thinks about how the story sounds when it is read out loud. Robert develops a story by talking instead of writing. To Robert, audience, **voice**, and revisions play important roles in story development.

Audience

Robert spends much of his time meeting the people who read his books. By talking to children, Robert can find out what they like to see or hear in a story. He learns what kinds of words they use when they talk. This helps him develop stories that interest children and use language that they understand.

Robert often gets ideas from the children he meets or letters they write to him.

Voice

To be a creative writer, an author has to have a unique way of presenting his or her story. Robert is known for using humor in his storytelling. He often uses words that some people do not think are proper, such as "peeing" and "underpants." These words help Robert reach his audience. This helps readers and listeners relate to the story he is telling.

Revisions

Robert's stories are rarely perfect when he first tells them. He often has to revise, or change, parts to get them just right. Robert bases the success of his stories on the reactions of his audience. If he is not getting the response he wants, he knows he has to rework the story until the characters, the plot, and the words all come together. Sometimes, it takes a long time for this to happen, but Robert feels it is worth the effort if the people reading and hearing his stories enjoy them.

Inspired to Write

Robert's children have served as the inspiration for four of his books. Julie is featured in both *Makeup Mess* and *David's Father*. Andrew is the main character in *Andrew's Loose Tooth*. *Something Good* was based on a junk-food phase Tyya went through.

■ Writing well is hard work and takes a great deal of practice.

Writing a Biography Review

A biography is an account of an individual's life that is written by another person. Some people's lives are very interesting. In school, you may be asked to write a biography review. The first thing to do when writing a biography review is to decide whom you would like to learn about. Your school library or community library will have a large selection of biographies from which to choose.

Are you interested in an author, a sports figure, an inventor, a movie star, or a president? Finding the right book is your first task. Whether you choose to write your review on a biography of Robert Munsch or another person, the task will be similar.

Begin your review by writing the title of the book, the author, and the person featured in the book. Then, start writing about the main events in the person's life. Include such things as where the person grew up and what his or her childhood was like.

You will want to add details about the person's adult life, such as whether he or she married or had children.

Next, write about what you think makes this person special. What kinds of experiences influenced this individual? For instance, did he or she grow up in unusual circumstances? Was the person determined to accomplish a goal? Include any details that surprised you.

A concept web is a useful research tool. Use the concept web on the right to begin researching your biography review.

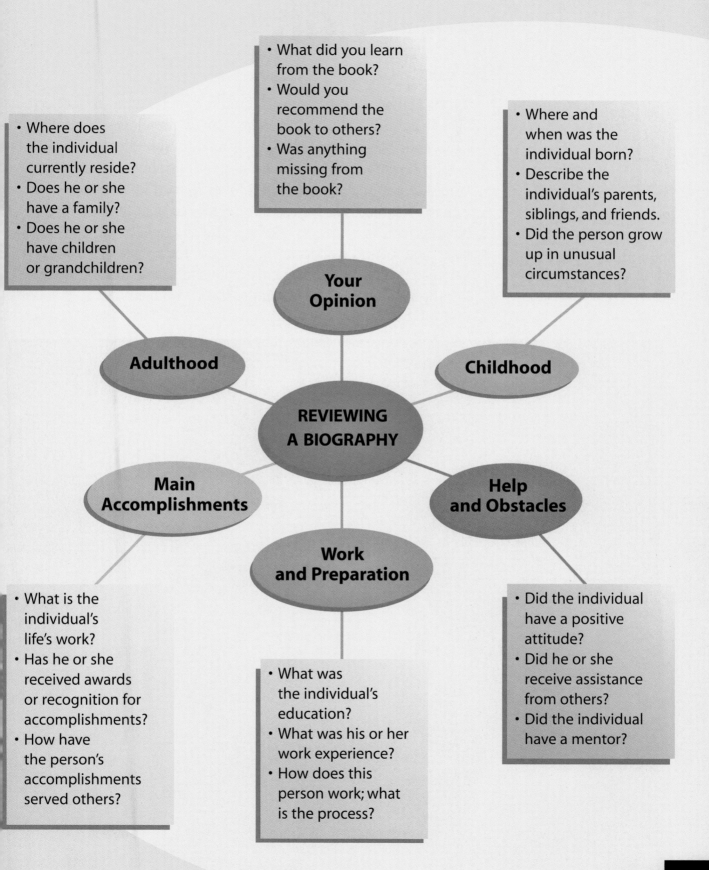

- Where does the individual currently reside?
- Does he or she have a family?
- Does he or she have children or grandchildren?

- What did you learn from the book?
- Would you recommend the book to others?
- Was anything missing from the book?

- Where and when was the individual born?
- Describe the individual's parents, siblings, and friends.
- Did the person grow up in unusual circumstances?

Your Opinion

Adulthood

Childhood

REVIEWING A BIOGRAPHY

Main Accomplishments

Help and Obstacles

Work and Preparation

- What is the individual's life's work?
- Has he or she received awards or recognition for accomplishments?
- How have the person's accomplishments served others?

- What was the individual's education?
- What was his or her work experience?
- How does this person work; what is the process?

- Did the individual have a positive attitude?
- Did he or she receive assistance from others?
- Did the individual have a mentor?

Fan Information

Each year, classrooms of children write letters to Robert Munsch. They tell him how much they love his books and which ones are their favorites. Sometimes, they ask Robert questions about writing and tell him how much they would like to meet him. Robert loves to read his fan mail and to meet his fans. He sometimes decides to visit the people that have written him letters. Teachers and students have been surprised to find Robert at their school for a visit. Once the surprise is over, Robert quickly settles in to tell stories, answer questions, and, most importantly, meet his fans.

■ Even though he is very busy, each year, Robert takes time to visit schools, sign books, and tell stories at theaters.

When Robert decides to visit a school or daycare, he often needs a place to stay. Instead of a hotel, he likes to stay with his fans and their families. **Raffles** are one way that the lucky family is chosen. While at their home, Robert spends as much time with the children as possible. They tell him their stories, and he tells them his. Robert gets new story ideas from many of these visits. Some of these children even get to be characters in his books.

Robert keeps in touch with fans through his website. Here, he posts information on his books, pictures from class and family visits, and artwork that some of his fans have sent him. People can even email Robert at the site.

WEB LINKS

Robert's Official Website

www.robertmunsch.com

To learn more about Robert, read unpublished stories, and see photos, visit Robert's official website.

Scholastic's Robert Munsch Website

www.scholastic.ca/titles/munsch

This site has information about Robert, his books, and class visits books.

Quiz

Q: Where was Robert Munsch born?

1

A: Pittsburgh, Pennsylvania

2

Q: Who was Robert's favorite author when he was growing up?

A: Dr. Seuss

3

Q: What did Robert plan to be when he graduated from high school?

A: A Jesuit priest

Q: Where did Robert and his wife meet?

A: At a daycare

Q: How many children do Robert and his wife have?

A: Three

Q: Who convinced Robert to start writing?

A: His boss and the boss's wife

Q: What was Robert's first published book?

A: Mud Puddle

Q: How many books has Robert written?

A: More than 40

Q: Which of Robert's books did the *New York Times* name the best-selling children's book of all time?

A: Love You Forever

Q: Where does Robert live?

A: In Ontario, Canada

Writing Terms

This glossary will introduce you to some of the main terms in the field of writing. Understanding these common writing terms will allow you to discuss your ideas about books and writing with others.

action: the moving events of a work of fiction

antagonist: the person in the story who opposes the main character

autobiography: a history of a person's life written by that person

biography: a written account of another person's life

character: a person in a story, poem, or play

climax: the most exciting moment or turning point in a story

episode: a short piece of action, or scene, in a story

fiction: stories about characters and events that are not real

foreshadow: hinting at something that is going to happen later in the book

imagery: a written description of a thing or idea that brings an image to mind

narrator: the speaker of the story who relates the events

nonfiction: writing that deals with real people and events

novel: published writing of considerable length that portrays characters within a story

plot: the order of events in a work of fiction

protagonist: the leading character of a story; often a likable character

resolution: the end of the story, when the conflict is settled

scene: a single episode in a story

setting: the place and time in which a work of fiction occurs

theme: an idea that runs throughout a work of fiction